ALL AROUND
Town

Please visit our web site at: www.garethstevens.com
For a free color catalog describing Gareth Stevens Publishing's
list of high-quality books and multimedia programs, call
1-800-542-2595 (USA) or 1-800-387-3178 (Canada).
Gareth Stevens Publishing's fax: (414) 332-3567.

Library of Congress Cataloging-in-Publication Data

Bontinck, Helga.
    All around town / Helga Bontinck.—North American ed.
      p. cm. — (Simple steps to drawing)
    Includes bibliographical references.
    ISBN 0-8368-6310-0 (lib. bdg.)
    1. Drawing—Technique—Juvenile literature. I. Title. II. Series.
NC655.B66   2006
741.2—dc22   2005040171

This edition first published in 2006 by
Gareth Stevens Publishing
A Member of the WRC Media Family of Companies
330 West Olive Street, Suite 100
Milwaukee, Wisconsin 53212 USA

This U.S. edition copyright © 2006 by Gareth Stevens, Inc. Original edition
copyright © 2005 by Creations for Children International. First published in 2005
by Creations for Children International, Belgium.

All illustrations by Helga Bontinck

Gareth Stevens editor: Dorothy L. Gibbs
Gareth Stevens designer: Scott M. Krall

Printed in the United States of America

1 2 3 4 5 6 7 8 9 10 09 08 07 06

Simple Steps to
Drawing

ALL AROUND
Town

GARETH**STEVENS**

GS PUBLISHING

A Member of the WRC Media Family of Companies

EASY DRAWING FUN

This book makes drawing easy, even for little hands. Each left-hand page shows you the shapes, lines, and figures you need to make the colorful drawing you see on the right-hand page. Three easy steps show you how to put the shapes together to make a drawing of a baker, a bicycle, a big truck, or any of six other people, animals, and objects you can find in or near a town.

All you have to do is copy the shapes you see in the first box in the order you see them in the boxes labeled 1, 2, 3. After you finish copying the shapes, you will have a simple drawing that you can color or paint to match the picture in the book — or any other way you like.

Get ready. Get set. **DRAW!**

WHAT YOU WILL NEED

For drawing, you will need a pencil and some sheets of plain paper.

A pencil with soft lead is the best kind for drawing. An ordinary No. 2 pencil will work well. If you use a pencil that is made specially for drawing, look for one marked HB. (H means hard lead. B means soft lead.) A pencil marked HB is not too hard and not too soft. Use plain white paper for your drawings. The colors and paints you will use to finish your pictures will show up best on white paper.

For coloring, you will need crayons, colored pencils, or markers.
For painting, you will need watercolors or acrylic or poster paints.

Crayons and colored pencils are easy to use and come in a wide range of colors. Markers and paints can be messy so you need to protect your clothing and your work area. If you want to paint your drawings, acrylic and poster paints work best because they dry quickly. You can have a lot of fun mixing paint colors. Even if you start with only red, blue, yellow, and black paints, you can mix them to make many other colors. Paintbrushes come in different thicknesses. You might want to have two brushes — a thin one and a thick one. Be sure to wash your brushes in water when you are finished painting.

Snowman

You will need all of these shapes and figures to draw this happy, well-dressed snowman.

1

2

3

6

Sunflower

Use the sunburst twice when you put these shapes together to draw a simple sunflower.

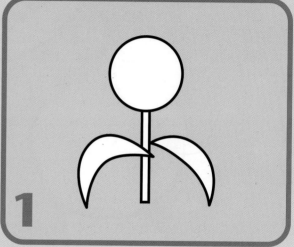

1

2

3

9

Baker

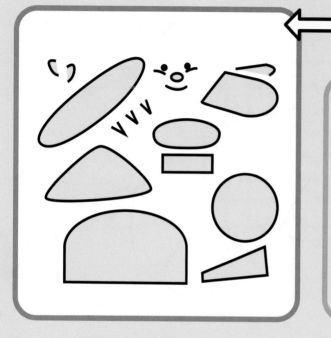

With these shapes and lines you can draw a busy baker and his bread.

1

2

3

11

Puppy Dog

Put these shapes and figures together to draw a perky pet puppy.

1

2

3

12

Tractor

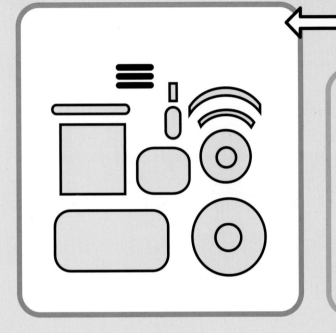

Circles, curves, and straight lines make up the figures you will need to draw a tractor.

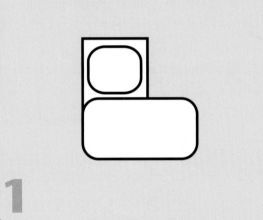

1

2

3

15

Fish Market

Draw these shapes to make a market stall, then just add fish, fruits, or any other foods.

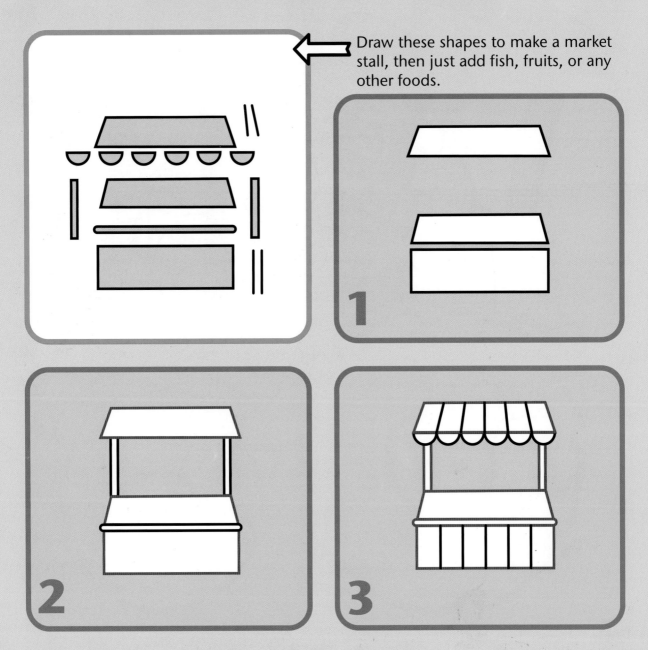

Birthday Cake

To make a birthday cake, you will have to draw most of these shapes and lines many times.

1

2

3

Bicycle

If you draw these shapes, lines, and figures in the right order, you can build a bike!

1

2

3

20

21

Big Truck

To build a truck, draw all the big shapes you see here, first, then add all the little shapes.

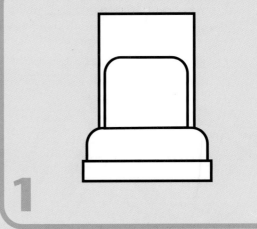

1

2

3

MORE EASY DRAWING FUN

Books

Dinosaurs. Easy to Read! Easy to Draw! (series).
    Joan Holub (Price Stern Sloan)

Drawing with Your Hands. Drawing Is Easy (series).
    Godeleine De Rosamel (Gareth Stevens)

I Can Draw Country Animals. I Can Draw Animals! (series).
    Hélène Leroux-Hugon (Gareth Stevens)

Let's Draw a House with Shapes. Let's Draw with Shapes (series).
    Jannel Khu (Rosen's PowerStart Press)

Web Sites

Draw and Color with Uncle Fred
www.unclefred.com

Learn to Draw: A Project 4 Kids
BillyBear4kids.com/Learn2Draw/Learn2Draw.html